Words For A Soul

Courtney Brooks - Leake

BookLeaf Publishing

Presentation by *BookLeaf Publishing*

Web: www.bookleafpub.com

E-mail: info@bookleafpub.com

ISBN: 9789357444392

First edition 2023

For all the souls who have been lost and found

Swim

Relationships sink
when you have the wrong people
in your boat
I'd rather swim
Then to have you be my anchor
and weigh me down

Reality

I hide behind my words
Because they're the only
Characters that can reveal
How I feel without acting

And Again

Take time to love yourself
Don't wear your worry on your sleeve
Don't allow the carelessness
Of someone else to make you feel defeat

They didn't love you
Although they claimed too
They left you broken
Weakened
And confused

But now you're getting over it
Because you found you

So dust off your heart
You still need it to love
Again
And again
And again

Depth

The depth of my love for you
Will make an ocean
Feel like a puddle

Homebody

I buried myself
In pajamas
Laziness
Lifetime tv
And sleep
I buried myself
Because I was comfortable
Being where I was
But today I decided
To find myself
Again
I curled my hair

I put on my favorite lipstick
Dressed up real nice
And went out
I always love home
Some days I forget I can
Leave it

Consumed

Society tells you beauty is enough
Maybe worth more than a degree
But how can I disagree
When a mug shot can get you
A modeling contract
Or nude photos can get
You a million followers on IG
You don't have to be talented
All that matters is how you look
Even if you are the best at what you do
You'll still get overlooked

Her Choice

If you can't carry life
Then you don't have a choice
On the matter of what a woman
Does with the life in her

Nature's Cry

When rain falls
It's mother nature's tears of sorrow
Weeping for the blood spilled upon her
The thunders echo with rage
  from shouting voices demanding justice
The sun shines light on inequality
Yet they appear to be blinded
Like they can't see when it's night

Motives

Some Men take women out on dates
Just so she can be
Dessert later
Some women accept the dates
Just to get a free meal
With no intentions
On ever calling
Each other back
After they both
Got what they
Wanted

Honey

Be mindful of the men
Who want to step out
To touch your precious jewel
Only to return back to
The flower they deviated
From after he gets
A taste of
Your honey

Ghosted

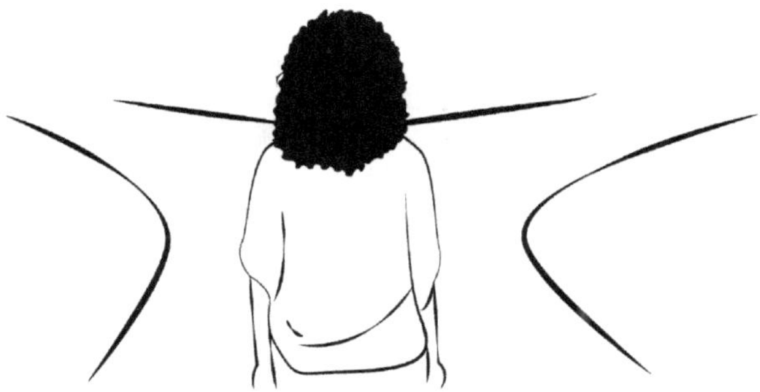

We live in a world
Where people claim
To be honest
Yet lack the courage
To tell you
They're not interested
Anymore

You are the Beholder

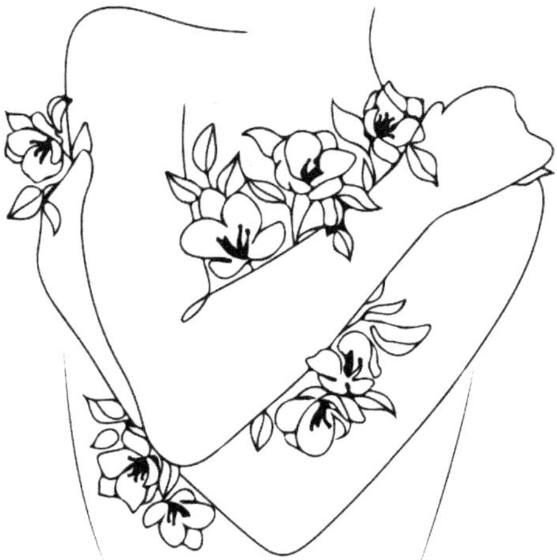

If you don’t think you’re beautiful
Its because you have been poisoned
By the words of others who tell
You what the definition of beauty is
Without realizing that you have
To define it yourself

Education in the USA

College costs you four years
And a lifetime of debt
Makes you wonder if its even worth
All that
There's no way you should do all the work
Then end up at Burger King just to work
As soon as you graduate
They're yelling pay me
As if six months is enough for a
Job guarantee
College is worth it
If you have the right connects
You have to have experience
Before you graduate

Because if you don't the career you want
May be a long wait
Don't allow reality to discourage you
College is amazing
But in America it should be free
Especially when the degree doesn't work for you
You have to do the work
For the degree

Cautious

I can’t be vulnerable around you
Because I'm afraid that if I pour
Out my heart
You wouldn’t have anything
To catch it with.

BS

His initials were BS
I find it funny
because that's exactly
what he was to me

Another Round of Love

I dusted off the memory box
In my mind
And I found you there
Its been a while since I've
Thought of you
But today I did
Its funny how one individual
Can determine how you will
Act with the next set of people
Who enter your life.

Step Into The Light

You've been in the dark for so long
Hidden by a love
That was never meant for you

Now you may step
Out into the sun
Stretch your arms
To the sky
Smile
Let the wind hit your face

You deserve to feel every ounce
Of freedom
You deserve a love that
Will shine bright
You were never meant
To be hidden

Love Dipped Lies

You see I only knew about love
From someone who claimed to
Love me
I had no experience
on my love resume
Because what he gave me
Wasn't it

Love
Be careful with that word
It sounds so sweet
Like Carmel covered candy apples
Or chocolate covered strawberries

When the words drizzle off of
Lying lips
Don’t believe everything you hear
Trust what you see
I love you
He said it so effortlessly
As he said it to her
And her
And her
And her
If I’d listened close enough
To the drizzled lies
I woudn’t have said
I love you too

Identity Theft

You can't give someone
all of you
when you are still trying
to figure out
who you are too

Fly Away

The entire time in the relationship
I was the caterpillar
Continuously growing
You were the tree stump
Standing still, never moving
What kind of love is that?
Luckily
I finally found out
How to use my wings

Flourish

Flowers bloom
The sun rises
Mountains reach their highest peaks
Balloons float
Grass grows
Trees stand tall as the sky
And darling if all these things
Can reach their maximum potential
Then certainly you can
Flourish high

www.ingramcontent.com/pod-product-compliance
Lightning Source LLC
Chambersburg PA
CBHW062110140826
49812CB00058B/1211
9789357444392